Children's Aid Direct has been wo[...] **1995 and in Albania since 1991.**

Those fleeing Kosovo include people who had been internally displaced for many months. As refugees they are crossing the border exhausted and in extreme need.

Children's Aid Direct has temporarily suspended its work in Kosovo and is now working in Albania and the Republic of Macedonia to give immediate assistance to thousands of refugees. Support also needs to be given to hosting communities, care centres, schools, homes as we continue with our existing aid programmes.

Children's Aid Direct expects to return to Kosovo at some stage to help rebuild communities with a special focus on child care services.

Voices for Kosovo will, it is hoped raise awareness, fundraising events, additional donations and support.

VOICES FOR KOSOVO
MUST BE HEARD AT THIS TIME

David H.W. Grubb
Executive Director, Children's Aid Direct
April 1999

Thank you for buying this book. Please introduce it to others. You could also use it to raise funds. All of the proceeds from this publication will benefit Children's Aid Direct as it continues to work in Albania, Macedonia, and in due course re-enters Kosovo.

Should you want to know more about the continuing relief situation, or about other members of the Disasters Emergency Committee, you are encouraged to contact:

Judith Egerton, Children's Aid Direct,
12 Portman Road, Reading RG30 1EA
Telephone 0118.958.4000
Fax 0118.958.8988
Website htttp://www.cad.org.uk
e-mail enquiries%cad@notesgw.compuserve.com

Registered charity no. 803236

Children's Aid *Direct*

Voices for Kosovo

edited by

Rupert Loydell

– Stride –

VOICES FOR KOSOVO
First edition 1999
© Stride 1999
ISBN 1 900152 64 9

Cover photos © Children's Aid Direct
Cover design by Neil Annat

Acknowledgements
Mark Dizdar's poems, translated by Francis R. Jones,
first appeared in *Kameni Spavač/Stone Sleeper* (Kuća bosanska);
'A text about the five' was also published in *Scar on the Stone* (Bloodaxe).
Aneta Benac Krstić's poems first appeared in *Scar on the Stone* (Bloodaxe).
'Chosen People' by Brian Louis Pearce first appeared in *Reform*
and was also published in *Leaving The Corner* (Stride).
'Picasso Is Right' by Penelope Shuttle first appeared in *Poesie Europe*
and was also published in *Selected Poems 1980-1990* (Oxford).
'Imagining the Worst' by Matt Simpson
was published in *Catching Up With History* (Bloodaxe).
Marko Vešović's 'Summa Summarum'
first appeared in *Scar on the Stone* (Bloodaxe).

Published by
Stride Publications
11 Sylvan Road, Exeter
Devon EX4 6EW
England

Contents

They sell us the President the same way
They sell us our clothes and our cars
They sell us everything from youth to religion
The same time they sell us our wars
I want to know who the men in the shadows are
I want to hear somebody asking them why
They can be counted on to tell us who our enemies are
But they're never the ones to fight or to die
And there are lives in the balance
There are people under fire
There are children at the cannons
And there is blood on the wire

— Jackson Browne, 'Lives in the Balance'

We are a feelingless people. If we could really feel, the pain
would be so great that we would stop all the suffering. If we
could feel that one person every six seconds dies of starvation
(and as this is happening, this writing, this reading, someone
is dying of starvation), we would stop it. If we could really feel
it in the bowels, the groin, the throat, in the breast, we would
go into the streets and stop the war, stop slavery, stop the
prisons, stop the killings, stop destruction. Ah, I might learn
what love is.

— Julian Beck, *The Life of the Theatre*

Inventing the Vocabulary

To put words in the right order. To order their truth. To respond to what the truth says to me. Perhaps to be astounded.

Whose words? Taken from fathers and mothers, from teachers, from those who mean beyond the normal meaning of words. Taken from poets and wordsmiths and cultivators of meaning and the political vocabulary and the priests who play with the music of words and the psychiatrist who takes the words out of the centre of your hands and heaps them on the table to be inspected.

There was one man where they put me who had been beaten near to death because of his use of words, his protests, his slogans. He gave them up. he *re-arranged* even his vocabulary. He began to speak in a new language and the other prisoners gradually learnt what he meant to say. A few of them were ever faster at inventing the vocabulary, the grammar, the structure than he was.

'Better to invent the vocabulary than it inventing you' they said between the self-imposed silences and the sounds of the new vocabulary that danced inside their skulls and made colour in their souls.

'Better to be silent than heard. Better to be without than accused. Better to invent a new world than have all the old world beaten out of you.'

Some of them said this as the ropes were applied, the wires were fixed or more simply the boot was put in where it hurt most.

Some of them said this as the police read back to them extracts from their diaries or letters or creative writing.

'Just what is this meant to mean?' Scream, scream.
'What on earth is one to make of this?' Scream, scream.
'Do you know what you are saying?'
'Is this what you really mean?'
'I can't believe my eyes.'

So cut out the tongue. So lop off the writing hand.
So pull out the eyes. So insert a rifle between the lips.
So blow the vocabulary to kingdom come.

So; what did you mean it to mean to say? What was your intention when you created this poem? Exactly what is the best way to read this? What have you to say for yourself?

Nowadays we all use different words. No more old songs. Soon nobody will be able to recite a line. The priests will have to learn that we have our own babble. The psychiatrist will see lying on the table top a pile of words that challenge every perception. Language that stands on its head. Words that do their own thing.

Now what am I to say and how are you to reply to me? What words?

Today, in the centre of the town where there was once a library and a school and a museum, there were two old men being beaten up by the police and there was frankly nothing out of the ordinary about that.

But then I recognised my father and my much older brother and I thought about attempting to assist them. That is assist the police. That is beat the two old men silly until they also had given up on words. This after all would have been the kindest thing to do.

When you think of joining the police to beat up your father and your brother what word might one use for this, this idea, this intervention, this concept?

Just what is the correct word for this?
Just what is the incorrect word for this?
Just what is the invented word for this?

The policeman has his word. My father and brother have another word. I start with silence and build up from there. I seek a new word that explains nothing. There is nothing to say about betrayal, treason, trickery.

I need a word for my wife, my mother, my soul.

If I had a new word for 'god' I would tell it more easily. I would confess.

Tonight do I say to my children there are no stories to tell or do I say from now on all stories will be new or do I begin to teach them about words?

What words?

Take this one. Say this one. Roll it on your mouth. Taste it. Say it over and over until it becomes pure sound. Then, gently re-invent it.

But even when you have done this, surely you can hear all the old associations and tones and texts sidling up like pimps, to do their thing again, to make it their own again.

Is prayer the purist form of communication or the purist form of confusion? Hah! Let me try that on you!

I write all this down in my mind. My mind's eye sees me doing this. What I am up to? I say 'no' to words and yet cannot trust the silence.

In my head I beat off the police, smother my father and brother with kisses, drag off the policemen's body and hurl it into the fountain, disappear into the night, feel brave, feel good, feel that I have won some sort of battle over evil.

But I do not do this and the words do not do this and I am left wondering what the word 'denial' needs to become.

Declare untrue. Disavow. Repudiate. Refuse. Statement of that thing is not true or existent.

When the policemen lay into the blood and bones of my father and brother what form of repudiation is this? What form of refusal? What statement?

When they brandish their metal sticks and hurl down the metal into the flesh what language do they hear in their own heads?

What story do they make up to send them to sleep that night?

What story do they believe in?

What words? What noises?

David H.W. Grubb

Events without Response

Soldiers are marching to war outside my window this sunny Saturday morning. There's column after column of them, with rifles slung across shoulders, drums beating; even a bagpiper leading the way. There are crowds on the street cheering & the flutter of bunting in the air.

In Torrington, North Devon, it's a beautiful spring day & there's about to be a battle.

But don't worry, there'll be no blood, no lost limbs, no grief for those 'lost', no desperate acts of heroism amongst the smoke & the shouts. The worst thing that might happen is the noise of the cannon making the small kids cry, or bad acting from the participants as they 'die'. It's 1646 again, & this Easter the Cavaliers & the Roundheads are being called up to celebrate the bank holiday, to celebrate the new '1646 Experience' Heritage Centre that's opening in the town today.

Soldiers are marching outside my window, marching down to the car park to go to battle. It feels surreal & strange. I wonder how many other battles in the English Civil War took place in car parks.

They've drawn a crowd here like you only see for the annual carnival, or on Mayday when children dance their coloured ribbons around the two Maypoles erected at either end of the Square. It's an event, a 'Family Day Out'.

This is war for recreation.

In my room, as the armies are passing, I turn on my computer, & check for mail.

Just a breaf helo from very stupid place to be. Slowly but surely I'll become as a vampire. Sleep by day and looking into sky by night. Situation is wors than you can imagine. Now they're bombarding 24 hours per day. But, I'm still alive and kicking. The thing that worry me the most is that with this bombing, all progressive power in my country will go in almost illegal existance. When this stupid war come to an end we will have to start over from zero. I hope here will be plenty job for your theatre workshop, but this will be very hard task even for you to find in people anything good. I hope that you are OK, and if there's any light in the end of the tunnel, please let me know, and for that I own you one good hangover.
Stay well. Max

and suddenly I feel stupid. I feel like I want to cry because of what seems in my head to be the insanity of what's happening outside in the light of the message on my screen.

But despite all these confused feelings, what I'm actually doing is smiling a big smile; I hadn't heard from Max in two days, & that can be a long time in Pristina.

•

I met Max in Norway. The drama company I work for, Wolf & Water Arts Co. has just spent three weeks in the Scandinavian snow, training a wide variety of groups – from school councils to Oslo Mediation Board – on the uses of theatre in conflict resolution. It's an area we specialise in, having wide experience of community arts work in Northern Ireland as well as work in prisons & mental health. We were the Theatre Company in residence at the European Conference of Peacemaking & Conflict Resolution last year, where the ties were forged that had brought us now to Norway.

Max was at the Nansen Academy in Lillehammer, a small organisation with centres in Norway & the Former Yugoslavia, which has been bringing together people from all sides of the conflict there into 'Dialogue Groups'. These are basically structured groups in which people from different ethnic backgrounds meet & talk & learn about each other – begin to see each other as individual people rather than the collective enemy & are therefore less likely to kill each other. This isn't as easy or 'nice' as it sounds; the groups are after all traditional enemies coming in angry & with many preconceptions. There are stories of how groups have literally had to be locked in rooms with each other until they talked.

Each academic term 12 or so Dialogue Group participants are taken from the balmy Balkans to icy Norway for a 10 week programme of Human Rights & Democracy training, learning ideas & skills to take back home with them & put into practice. We were doing a two-day piece of training, preparing one such group to return home at the end of the week, on how to put some of the theory they had learnt into practice.

We meet the group in their workroom. There's a range of people; Mentor, who's an ethnic Albanian actor from Pristina; Drita, an ethnic Albanian journalist from Kosovo; Mona, a Serb school teacher from Pristina; Didka, an aid worker from Skopje; 'Mad' Yasha, a medical student; Boris the computer wizard; & so on. And then there's Max, a Serb from Pristina.

Now, however democratic one tries to be doing drama with people, every group always has its stars & Max is this group's star. Shambling & short, he looks like a long haired Robert De Niro; we strike up a rapport on the very first evening we arrive, as he bums a cigarette off us just as we are about to go off into Lillehammer to have a mosey & buy some post cards.

On the card he gives me it reads:

Dejan Marjanovi   Max
advisor

'Advisor': that's a great description for Max. He would, at the drop of a hat, proceed to give you advice with a laconic enthusiasm on just about any topic you'd care to bring up. Politics, women, sport, the price of beer... all with constant shrugs of the shoulder & 'I don't know, don't ask me why these things are true' hand gestures.

'Lillehammer? Let me tell you about Lillehammer', he says. 'Go outside & walk maybe 20 metres. Look around, because it's really beautiful. And then come back cos that's all there is. It's a hole. A beautiful hole, but a hole. Welcome to downtown Lillehammer!' He lights the cigarette he's been given & walks off.

When we come to work with the group the next morning, it's good, but hard work. Not because they're reticent like some groups are doing drama for the first time, in fact it's almost the opposite. We do our usual medley of fun, energising warm up games & exercises & they're almost bouncing around on the ceiling. They love the masks we bring out & just start playing & laughing with them. During one of the breaks Max explains this behaviour as just being 'The Balkan Temperament', but we're not so sure. It's giddier than that. Sue puts her finger on it when she describes it as being like 'gate fever'.

Gate Fever is a phenomenon that happens with inmates just before they leave prison. We've experienced it with such groups while doing theatre as part of pre release programmes. It's a kind of almost childlike sense of anticipation – such excitement at the prospect of release that they have trouble holding that excitement. But at the same time that excitement is given an edge by a sense of fear, of not knowing what it's going to be like once they get out & what exactly the future holds. Will they get a job? What will it be like with family & mates? Will they re-offend again?

13

It was a version of this mix of expectation & apprehension that we were seeing in the behaviour of this group, as they thought about returning home.

'I am sick of snow', says little Blerina. 'I like snow when it comes in my country, but then it goes. Here that's all there is.'

'And the beer is so expensive', moans Max. 'In my country it is only the equivalent of two kroner.' We do some maths & that works out at about 40p.

Greeny, the big Serb skinhead from Belgrade who cites *Blackadder* as one of the most important influences on his life complains about the food here; when it's lunchtime & we are faced with two options of two equally delicious dishes – either raw sticks of carrot floating in large bowls of water or raw slices of swede floating in large bowls of water – we tend to concur.

After ten weeks away people are really missing friends & family (not to mention decent weather, decent beer & decent food). In the breaks in our sessions people crowd around the computer in the corner of the room, fighting to get to their Hotmail for news from home.

Things back home don't seem good. There is a further NATO deadline in place that runs out two days hence. The group are worried but tend to dismiss it, maybe because one deadline has already come & gone, & maybe because that's the easiest thing to do in the face of the alternative being threatened.

It's hard but good with the group. At the end of the first day we know that we've won them over. They're having a good time, & finding what we do interesting & useful, which is always gratifying.

In the evening the whole group take us out for a beer in Zippers bar in Lillehammer (it's 'cheap night' – a pint is only about £3.50 a shot). Max & I play pool. As he's winning, I resort to a snooker. He plays the shot off the cushion & hits one of my balls & I, delighted, thank him for two shots. Max is astonished, & with big pleading eyes tells me how in Pristina, the rule if you're snookered is that you can hit any ball, even your opponents, provided that the white comes off the cushion. 'But no, never mind, my mistake, my mistake – we will play your UK rules', he keeps telling me, in such a way that we adopt the Pristina rules for the rest of the evening. And maybe I'll never know unless I actually go to Pristina whether he was blagging me or not.

It's the second day & having identified the mentality of the group, we know a bit more how to play it. I start off by putting on a mask & becoming a character, Ivar, playing someone who could be part of the group. Jon & Sue facilitate the rest of the group in asking me questions about what I'm going to do, how I'm going to put my character's experience for the last 10 weeks in the Nansen Academy into use once I get home. In doing so I try to have Ivar voice some of the fears & uncertainties that members of the group must be going through in their own heads.

It's a simple exercise that cracks open where the group is; 'I have learnt a lot & changed my attitudes through being here', says Drita, 'but my family, my friends have not. I don't know where to begin in trying to change them & their attitudes. If I did they would regard me as a traitor. Yes, I want to see them – they are my family & friends, but I don't know what I can do.'

The group start acting as their own therapists, their own advisors. There is the acknowledgement that they are probably not going to change the entire situation in a week, a year, maybe a lifetime. That they are part of a slow, slow drip by drip effect – & that that position is a very lonely & potentially dispiriting one. Max, as his card says, advises; he seems suddenly very real, very wise, very honest: 'I can change no one. Only people can change themselves. Maybe I can help that change by the way I behave, the way I act, by what I say. But I can only be sure of myself. I know here I have met people who I am told should be my enemies & I like them. That's a good thing to share with others. And ultimately I know that whatever happens I will not fight; that that's where I draw the line.'

The final scenes we do at the end of the day are getting people to present short pieces of theatre that show the smallest problem they might have to face on their return home. There are three stories, two of which are about trying to communicate with friends & family the ideas & the concepts that group members have experienced at Nansen. And there's a scene of simply trying to get through a checkpoint & being interrogated. Max plays the Passport Control Officer character at the checkpoint. He plays it as an utter bastard, a bastard who knows that they have power & all the time in the world to exercise it in the smallest of ways: a look, a cough, a telephone call. It's an electric piece of theatre.

We forum each of the scenes – a process in which the audience suggest & try out different solutions to the problems on stage. All the solutions come down to the ability to create empathy, of listening & accepting & persuading. Human contact, nothing more special than that.

It's the end of the second day & the group has worked hard. In the feedback they seem really happy with what we've done with them. 'I have never seen so many people from this course so into what they're doing', says one. 'This has been the most useful part of our time here', says another. I'm recording the feedback comments on my Walkman placed in the centre of the circle. Max is last: 'I have had a good time. A useful time. You are very welcome in my country whenever you come. We need you. And if you come, I can promise you wine, women & bombs.' When I switch the praise-engorged Walkman off at the end of the feedback, Max says 'So, can we talk honestly now?' & everyone laughs.

·

We're in Oslo for a week, still working. A city with far more bustle than Lillehammer. I'm staying with my friend Lone (pronounced 'Lunar') Pålshaugen who is herself a brilliant conflict resolution facilitator, & principally the main person who is responsible for us being in Norway. Two weeks previously we had both been working up in Trondheim at the Isfit International Conflict Resolution Festival, where she too has been working with a Former Yugoslavian dialogue group. We compare notes & in the evenings huddle on her sofa & watch BBC News as deadlines pass & the NATO threats get more pronounced, the rumble of possible war louder.

A week to the day after we have left Nansen, we get a phone call from Steinar Brynn, the Academy's director. Most of the group he tells me has, in the light of the current uncertainty, decided to stay in Norway for the time being, to see how things unfold. Would we come back & do some more work with them?

It's only Jon & me who go back to Lillehammer, Sue has already returned to the UK to fulfil other work commitments. It's a very different group that we return to. Max, Didka & some of the others have returned to their homes. Those that are left are no longer the skittish group we worked with a week earlier; the excitement has gone & all that's left is the anxiety.

The next three days work are some of the hardest I've ever undertaken. I work with resistant groups, aggressive groups, groups who don't really see the point in what you're doing – but this is a different kind of negative energy, one which is about uselessness, powerlessness, hopelessness. At times it is like working in some alien, poisonous atmosphere that robs you of the will even to want to make an effort. We get the group flowing on some exercise or another with such effort – really pushing the proverbial boulder up the proverbial hill – but then in the breaks, group members cluster around the TV, around the internet, grim faced, waiting for news. Despair moths, worry junkies.

News comes in on mobile phones of two incidents in Pristina; a machine gun attack & a bombing at café & a bar. As, within hours, casualty lists of the dead & injured appear on the internet, group members from Pristina recognise names. We're looking for Max's, but it isn't there. Mentor steps back from the computer screen repeating 'I don't believe it, I don't believe it' over & over to himself. A friend of his & Blerina's is one of the dead. Later that evening he tells me, with tears in his eyes, of Adrianna, aged 22, an actress he had worked with. 'She was so full of life', he says. 'You could hear her laugh from the other side of a crowded bar & know she was there.' Mentor is really struggling to keep everything together. Pristina is a small city, he tells me, & The Magic Café is the main young people's place. 'If I had been in Pristina last night, that's where I would have been; Blerina too', he explains.

On our first day of work after our return, we try & create some theatre that will in someway reflect their current experience. We set up what turns into an almost Beckett-like scene of a waiting room, where there are no time tables & people are scared & bored. It's a brilliant scene, but the group literally gets stuck in it, unable to move beyond it what ever we try out or suggest. It's like watching conditioned helplessness in small children; it's very scary.

It's difficult to know what on earth we can offer. We can't change anything that is happening, we can't raise the dead. As the first pictures of the bomb attack aftermath come through on CNN, members of the group recognise friends among the images of casualties. These people who last week thought that they were returning home, are now disconnected from their own futures. They cannot return home (flights have stopped to Belgrade & Pristina) & they feel guilty about that fact; guilty & worried about friends & family back there. Meanwhile, visa time in Norway is ticking away & nobody, not even Steinar, seems to know what they will do.

In the end we stop trying to be psychologically clever & just do what we can do: theatre. Playing silly games to help pass the time, to make people laugh. We try using different rooms to the one with the TV & the Internet in which we have been using, to see if we can break the morbid modality. We start using video so that people can dip in & out of the work, so they can do what they need to do & join in as they feel fit & able to engage. It works, but only in fragments. I have never felt so paralysed. Steinar, a big man who looks like Father Christmas must have when he was 40, gently tells us that we are serving an important function just by being here, just by caring.

In one of the games I am grabbed by Greeny who gives me a big happy hug. Greeny is neither a small nor a weak man; in fact he fractures my rib. I feel privileged to be a victim of Serb affection as opposed to all the Serb aggression that the media is full of.

There is an announcement. Steinar is taking us all out for the evening. The whole of the remaining Balkan group – me & Jon, & a large selection of the Norwegian students who are also at the Nansen Academy. We head out to a bar in Lillehammer, & all sit around a big table, 20 odd of us, & Steinar buys the drinks. And keeps buying the drinks. And keeps buying the drinks, until everyone is so hammered that we can barely walk. 'The bombing will start tomorrow' one of the group tells me. I wonder if they've received news that I haven't yet heard? 'How do you know?' I ask. 'Because Steinar is buying us all these drinks. He knows, he knows.'

Walking back carefully on the ice & snow I ask Steinar if he does know. He smiles gently & tells me 'I know because of the weather forecast – there has been fog over Belgrade for the last three nights. Tonight on the forecast they said it had cleared – that's what NATO have been waiting for.' As we walk on he says 'If I had the money I would buy pubs all over the former Yugoslavia – 40 pubs, that's all it would take – & I'd get everyone in there & buy them all drinks & get them talking to each other instead of fighting each other.'

The next morning, the very hung over group has to deal with an anticipated flood of journalists. NATO has said they intend to bomb, it is now just a matter of when. And Norwegian hacks, looking for a local angle, looking for some real life Serbs & Ethnical Albanians to interview, have woken up to the Nansen Academy. TV crews jostle through. A journalist sits down in front of the group & Greeny says 'Please, I'd ask you one thing – not to ask us how we feel about the bombing. It is our parents, our brothers & sisters, our friends back there. It is a stupid question.'

In this chaos I leave. Jon is going to stay, but I need to get back to Oslo to work with another group. And I need to get away from all of this madness. I actually need to talk to someone about this who's on the outside & who will understand. In this case that's Lone. And for once, I actually just need a hug.

Just as I'm leaving the first news of missile strikes against Belgrade & Pristina are coming through on CNN & we all stand, in an awesome silence, watching the TV, while behind us the television crew films. When I try & say goodbye to each person in the group I don't know what to say.

Visar from Pristina says as we hug goodbye 'You will not forget us, will you?' It is one promise I can make at least.

Blanchot, writing about the Holocaust, talked about the idea of the 'event without response' – meaning an event or situation that is so powerful that no response can express or encapsulate its totality. I didn't realise that this could apply to goodbyes as well. I slip away.

·

I remember sitting on the train back to Oslo, watching the monochrome landscape of snowy fields & black trees, feeling dead. Where the white sky meets the white surface of the frozen lake the train track follows, there is only whiteness, there's no horizon to be seen. That state of being so tired that one feels a risk to oneself & others. That kind of tiredness that you know not even a good night's sleep is going to sort out.

I get back & Lone has received an e-mail from Besnik, a young guy from Belgrade who was part of the dialogue group in Trondheim. A missile has hit nearby & his best friend has been killed. It appears that targets around Pristina are also being attacked. We sit & watch the news as it flows in. How long can you string out the simple fact that the bombing has started in a news report? Virtually endlessly, so it seems. Lone is knitting & I'm drinking beer & we're both thinking of our friends: Filip & Besnik in Belgrade, Eli, Violeta & Max in Pristina. On TV2 we catch the news report that was filmed from the Nansen Academy – the ghostly shot of people standing & watching the news on the television as I left. There's Greeny & Drita talking about their fears, talking about the Nansen Academy & its work in reconciliation & peace building. At the end of the piece they hug; perfect TV.

The next news item is a report from an ethnic Albanian community centre somewhere in Oslo, with lots of men sitting & watching the news of the bombings. The difference is that they cheer.

Back in the UK I feel even more at sea now. I am not a politician & I'm not running for office & I have no idea about the rights & wrongs of this situation that my country is embroiled in. Filip, my friend in Belgrade told me once that he'd stopped telling people where he was from, he simply didn't want to define himself in that way; 'I am a citizen of the world' he will tell you. I'm just very selfishly worried about my friends, Serb, ethnic Albanian, Macedonian.

I have spent the last few weeks constantly listening to the news, firing e-mails into the darkness, for what it's worth. It feels a tiny tiny gesture. And better than firing Tomahawk missiles at least.

What does one do? Filip told me another story about when he was working with refugees in Croatia. He was supervising a food queue – hundreds of people standing for hours to get not enough food. He described the dejection, the despair on peoples faces. Suddenly, this VW van draws up along side the queue & two clowns jump out & just start doing their silly act up & down the queue. Filip described how the atmosphere was transformed, how people started laughing & chatting with each other as they watched. After an hour the clowns jumped back in their van & disappeared. Apparently they called themselves Clowns without Frontiers. The good atmosphere lasted quite some time in the queue; it made a little difference. Just like what we did at Nansen did, I suppose. I find it so easy to be laid low by what is happening; it is too much to try & respond to 'events without response'. It is possible though, to do something small; a conjuring trick, an e-mail, buying this book. And those small acts of kindness should never be underestimated.

Of my friends, Filip has escaped to Budapest from Belgrade after going into hiding; there was the worry that because he'd been involved in cross-community peace building projects that he might be arrested as a collaborator. Violeta, a lovely 50 year old woman who is like your favourite aunt escaped from Pristina & walked to & across the Macedonian border, where she has stayed to help with the flood of refugees. And then those who we haven't heard from in a while. Eli in Pristina – a beautiful young woman, sharp & witty & hard. And Besnik now seems to have become silent too. And while it's not time to despair yet, I do not know into what darkness these two young people may or may not have fallen, & I can feel my eyes fill up as I think of them.

And Max. Good old Max. Max is still in Pristina, in his apartment, avoiding getting drafted into the Serbian army & holding true to his principles of non-violence. We e-mail each other regularly; his friend Goran is holed up with him. I tell Goran to make sure that Max changes his underwear on a regular basis. Goran writes back that he definitely will – that the bombings are one thing, Max not changing his knickers would truly make Pristina a hellhole.

Dear Peter

This is Max (and Goran, as you used to) speaking from free Yugoslavia. Two bad Serbs are in the one room – save yourselves and your shelves.

Thank you (again) for your concern about our destiny. One day we hope we will return it when NATO start bombing your town (God forbid). News are that centre of Pristina is heavily damaged (almost destroyed) in yet another NATO's firecracker three nights ago. I am in a sort of ilegal position (he don't go out from his apartment if it's not really, really, neccesary) because they want me to join the army (and, what the army it will be), and they want it really bad.

I hope we will play soon one more snooker game, and drink some beers with normal prices (less than fortune).

(Goran is in brackets)

Stay well.

Max & Goran

Two regular blokes in the middle of a war.

I e-mail Max, telling him that on this sunny Saturday morning, that there's an army marching, that there's a make-believe battle about to take place in my town, & explain to him about the Civil War reconstruction.

He e-mails me back straight away. He thinks it's a great idea & wonders if we could get something together to recreate the battle of Pristina sometime. But then, he reckons, NATO will probably do it tonight anyway.

Peter Harris

Kosovo/a – 1996

Denials and Dreams

Kosovo/a borders Albania and Macedonia. It is situated in the south east of the Federal Republic of Yugoslavia and is considered to be one of the least developed regions in Europe. The capital is Pristina; 90% of the people are Albanian, the rest are Serbian. Kosovo is the Serbian spelling; Kosova is the Albanian spelling. The difference is of immense political, historical and symbolic significance.

The Serbian minority dominates the Albanian population, most of the Albanians are unemployed, double sanctions depressed the economy further and raised ethnic tensions. Since August 1995 refugees from Krajina have compounded an already existing refugee problem. Thousands of children are growing up in a land where equality is but an idea.

The economy is not designed to deliver welfare provisions equally. A very small Serbian minority prosper within the economy and rule it. 90% strive outside with their own alternative provisions; these are the Albanians. No economy could possibly sustain such a situation for long. It is a political strategy and there is no secret at all about this. Kosovo/a is existing on a challenge of ethnic wills.

Protection, nutrition, healthcare, education and recreation are not available to thousands of children in Kosovo/a. For the ethnic minority this creates a constant tension whilst also manufacturing an idealistic concept of Albania and unification. Such denial, such suppression, is of particular significance when children comprise just under half of the total population (2 million) and where Albanians have large families.

Maternity leave, child allowances, pre school facilities, assistance with disabled children and education generally are not easily available or available at all for Albanian families.

When in 1990 Belgrade imposed a new Serbian curriculum the Albanian teachers were sacked, even attacked and in due course they created their own schools and universities in private homes. This 'parallel' system works, despite the fact that electricity, heating and materials have had to be provided by the Albanians and this has often been beyond their resources. A 'parallel' system that also stretches to health and recreation and organised sports, however, reveals the desperate nature of this divide...

At school, in the street, at work and out of work the demarcation dominates life.

The arrival in August 1995 of refugees from Krajina added to the tension. Over 13,000 refugees had to be accommodated. Some have found employment. They are separated from the Albanian community and most live in collective centres. The collective experiences, aspirations and individual motivations of these refugees add to the ethnic tension.

Kosovo/a has a weak manufacturing industry and agriculture. It was poor before the war and sanctions and the arrival of new refugees. Albanians and also Serbs are unemployed; professional people have become the new poor.

42% of the population is linked to unsafe water supplies. There have been frequent water and power supply cut offs. Sewage systems are extremely crude. Nutrition is poor and under nourishment of children and mothers is evident. Infections are endemic and up to now vaccination schemes have not been satisfactory. Primary health care is fragile to non existent.

The denial of the most basic care systems to so many, a denial created by politics and ethnic dispute as well as war sanctions and displacement, has created a world of parallel struggles, parallel limitations, parallel failures in Kosovo/a. The sense of being trapped, of boycotting is very evident when observing and meeting the Albanians. The Serbian population must feel even more uncertain; despite the iron rule and the threat, the absence of a logical objective and of development must be equally apparent. People cannot eat politics. Dreams do not provide clean water. A vision of Albania cannot heat a home. Children are dying from frequent epidemics that could be avoided.

One of the major problems in perception relating to Pristina, the capital city, and Kosovo/a itself is that history and the Balkans and Bosnia are used to define it rather than more simple references to geographical location and type. Kosovo/a is a southern province within a republic. There are 1448 villages and the capital is quite unlike them.

When there is power, at night Pristina glows dramatically giving a totally false picture of wealth and status; as do the cafes and night-clubs and civic buildings. This image is partially created because so many people live in high rise apartments (the old dwellings went in the 1950's as part of a purge on all that was old). In daylight these apartments might remind one of Bulgaria.

Old men wear the white skull cap, partly one suspects as an act of Albanian defiance and in late September orchards are heavy with pears and plums and quinces. Refuse is dumped on street corners yet everywhere there are people sweeping shop fronts and pavements. The restaurants are friendly and clean.

Pristina of course is not Kosovo/a. In the villages there are very different scenes. It is to some degree an oasis, a watering place in an unhappy land, best at night with the bright lights, an extraordinary contrast to the daily grind.

In Pristina Bosnia seems a world away and the dream of Tirana strangely close.

Children with Disabilities

There could be as many as 23,000 disabled children in Kosovo/a. Because of the political/economic context few of them have social protection or provision, they are totally dependent on their families. What support associations did exist in the 1980's have mostly ceased due to lack of financial support. The rights of the disabled hardly exist.

Gëzim is eight years old. Ten years ago his family moved to Pristina from a nearby village because there was no school for the children in that village. When he was four years old Gëzim was very ill. His mother said that he had an extremely high temperature. After the illness there was some problem with his speech and then with walking. His legs began to bow. Land was sold to pay for Gëzim to visit a specialist in Germany. The parents and grandparents are tremendously supportive of Gëzim and take him to a centre run by volunteer parents. There is, however, no dedicated and ongoing support for Gëzim because he is Albanian. His current and future care will be extremely limited. No wheel chair or crutches or other equipment is currently available. Despite the good intentions of the adults, Gëzim is growing more dependent and possibly there are the beginnings of social deprivation.

Gëzim's younger brother is now beginning to have walking problems it appears. He has not been to a doctor. It will cost 80 DMS. Attitudes, politics, logistics get in the way. The mother says she will take him to the doctor but she needs assistance and support. In reality Gëzim and his brother and the family are left to provide as best they can.

The mother has three children to care for. The husband sometimes has work. Their small home stands on a hillside at the end of a crude track. The interior replicates a typical Albanian cottage and Gëzim is loved and protected by his family. The cold winters, the lack of regular income, the threat of ethnic hatred, lack of medical help, all major challenges. The risk of more serious illness is considerable.

Genc also lives in Pristina. His parents are teachers and for three years received no pay so had to rely on the support of relatives. They, unlike some, did not have money provided by relatives living abroad.

Genc is 9 years old. There are two older children. He had a normal birth and after four months a high temperature and stomach problems. He is diagnosed as a Downs Syndrome child. He has been to Zagreb and also Belgrade for examinations. He didn't walk until he was five years old.

Genc cannot do anything to help himself in terms of eating, dressing and using the toilet. He requires constant attention throughout the day but sleeps well at night. His parents are extremely well educated and adore Genc but the strain is evident and both they and Genc need support. Because Genc is an Albanian child, that support will have to be fought for. The system will get in the way. He will suffer as all 'parallel' children do. Genc is outside the system.

Genc attends a centre set up by volunteers. He needs in particular speech training and to mix with other children. He might in time be able to attend school as a special needs pupil but the level of care and specific treatment required is hardly likely to be met.

The love of his parents and care of his family overall is enough currently to protect Genc. When he is older, what will happen to him? It is *now* that Genc needs the training and his parents special support.

Alvina is five years old. She suffers from cerebral palsy. She lives in Mitrovica, an industrial centre about forty minutes drive from Pristina.

Alvina's twin brother is perfectly healthy but Alvina is extremely frail and she has very specific needs. Her mother and father battle to provide for her and indeed her mother has learnt to give physiotherapy three times a day. Depending on how Alvina is, this can take hours.

Specialist advice and care is available but not for Alvina, she too is Albanian and the system does not support her. Her mother and the voluntary group at the Centre are rich support systems but naturally limited in what they can provide. Alvina, therefore, has a limited life and a totally uncertain future.

Another family also lives in Mitrovica. They own no home, they receive no income; they rent what they can supported by the mother's relatives. The three children and the father are blind.

The father, speaks some English and has received training but cannot get employment. He is wonderfully attentive to his three blind children and his wife who somehow provides food and clothing and keeps the family together. Some limited humanitarian agency support is what keeps them alive.

The eldest was born in 1992, the middle child in 1994 and the youngest in 1995. A one year sponsorship by some Italians is about to end. The diagnosis for the children is congenital cataracts and there could be a possibility of either surgery or treatment if the family could pay to get to a specialist. The family, however, is Albanian and lives on the edge and despite the support of a local volunteer centre is rapidly declining. Nobody has any idea what will happen when the money from Italy ceases. The property is very basic and despite the mother's monumental efforts the risk of accident or disease is high. In Kosovo/a, however, there is no red button to push, no 'phone to pick up, no support waiting. This family is in crisis. Many children in this community are at risk and their parents are under massive strain to make ends meet.

Life is a struggle, that is taken for granted. The existence of a disabled child means that extra resources are called for and if you are poor, unemployed, Albanian and in Kosovo/a the test is extreme. These children are failing because their rights are not recognised by any welfare system.

Refugees within Kosovo/a

When the refugees from Krajina came to Kosovo/a they created entirely new problems and added to the economic strain; there were 13,617 of them. Whilst some have been offered employment, most of the refugees would have expected their stay to be temporary and brief at that. Many would have anticipated staying in Belgrade. In every way Kosovo/a was a surprise.

There are over 150 Collective Centres. A small number of refuges are living in private accommodation. They receive aid from several agencies but never enough and naturally many of their needs are of a different nature.

Mothers and babies are those with special needs (as well as the elderly and disabled). The mothers need to keep healthy to support their children. Their diet is low on vitamins and hygiene items are very much needed, especially for babies.

In addition to basic materials and depending on the state of the centre, a large number of these refugees will experience dislocation, loss, a sense of threat. One wonders what information base they work on, what special care for trauma and stress is required, what longer term problems might arise.

The children, of course, provide a specific focus for Children's Aid Direct. What sense of security do these children now have? Their nutrition has been reduced and basic healthcare is indeed basic. What of their educational and recreational needs?

The presence of so many refugees from a different culture creates not only additional tensions but another spectrum of growing need that Kosovo/a is quite unable to respond to alone.

At the Arhiv Grada centre in Pristina, one of 38 centres in the city and nearby, we meet a family of four. There are two girls aged four and two and they attend kindergarten each day.

They come from Vukovar and fled in August 1995. The simple room in the centre is free. The father worked as a journalist for a while but receiving no pay he gave up. He would like to sell some of his paintings but it is difficult.

The room is small. They are supplied with food each day from a central kitchen but and they would rather be supplied direct and cook their own. There has been no supply of hygiene materials for months.

They need clothes, shoes, jackets for the children. There are twenty two children in this centre, from 7 years to 13 years old. There are also two babies. 50 people in all live here.

In terms of nutrition and health the food is limited. The children are anaemic. There is an obvious vitamin deficiency.

They wash their clothes in the showers and dry them in the single room. They purchase their own soap powder. They need to look after their money very carefully because the future is totally unknown.

This family is Serbian. They find it ludicrous that they are refugees in Serbia. They do not wish to see Vukovar ever again. They simply cannot believe that they are refugees within Serbia. They are keen to point out that real peace between people will come, but it will take some time. They ask us to understand.

Who knows how it may end?

On May 1st all of the school children used to come to the park on the outskirts of Pristina to experience the woods and fresh air. Now the swimming pool has been drained for the winter and there is tarmac where there were tracks and refugees occupy many of the houses. Entering the park there is a small Serb restaurant. People still come here to get away from the pressure of traffic and city life. There are pine trees and grazing cows and park benches and a view of distant mountains.

My guide tells me how he used to run in the park. He feels less inclined now. Each day he and his family watch two hours of television news from Albania because it is about their culture and Kosova. He ruminates about how the Albanians in Kosova feel, their dislocation, their desire to be appreciated in Europe, the pressure that double sanctions inflicted upon them, the grinding poverty. He refers to the older pupils who work so hard, dress well and seek the bigger world but who don't want to live abroad; they desire their own life and culture here. After lessons there is homework. Then if it is fine they will walk in the city between the bright lights. It takes about 20 DMS to kit up for school and they don't earn money in their spare time. They walk and talk but don't have the money to spend. City life looks good but close up it is different. Take away the bright lights or wander into the poor areas and the villages and there is a stark reality of struggle and cultural defiance. Who knows how it may end? The coming winter will test them all again.

Children's Aid Direct

Children's voices from Kosovo

I live with 7 members of my family and conditions in my family are very bad. I go to primary school and we are trying to learn well because school is knowledge. Our school is lacking every means for learning.

I give my greetings to all the children of the world.

Arbenita (11 years)

I live with my family of 17 members. Nobody in my family can get work. Very often we don't have bread on the table and as I am at school I'm very often lacking notebooks and pens.

Although we live in bad conditions, we find time and possibilities to learn. Our teachers come into the classroom with old clothes because their conditions are very bad as well.

In our classrooms we are often without chalk and we don't have any heating. But our teachers have a great will to teach us so we have a great success.

We decided to overcome our situation. Our love for education and thirst for freedom is enormous.

I wish that children all over the world will not have my kind of childhood. I wish them and their familes to be happy.

Arberije (14 years)

There are eight people in our family and our house only has two rooms. In the winter we cannot warm them and I can't sleep from the cold. My brothers and I are trying to earn some money working in the market but it is difficult because we are so little. We are not like other children because we live in very hard conditions of poverty.

Argon (14 years)

Conditions in my family are very bad. There are ten of us and I don't have a house. We live in only one room. We eat and sleep there. We don't have good meals, only simple ones.

When I go out in the city I don't see happy children.

Arjetta (14 years)

There are seven people living in our house. My parents cannot get a job and only my grandmother has a pension of 22DM per month. What can we buy with 22DM? We need 100kg of flour per month and that costs 50DM.

Naser (15 years)

In the beginning my life was not so difficult but then I had to start thinking about my future. What will tomorrow bring? Will the situation always be as bad as now or will we have a better life?

Why can't I be like other children and dream about playing. Instead I must think 'Will we have bread for tomorrow so that we can survive?'

I give my greetings to the whole world and all the children. I wish them all the best and in my dreams I see us smiling.

Rita (14 years)

My family's conditions are very bad. Nine of us live together and only my grandfather works. My grandmother is ill and she is always in bed so we must help her to do everything.

My brother is in 8th grade and I also have 3 little sisters. Two are in school and one is 4 years old. We all go to school and we love it as our home. Our friends we consider as brothers and sisters and our teachers as father and mother.

Very often we don't have chalk in our school but we are determined to learn. It is very difficult to live like this.

Shkurte (13 years)

There are ten members in the family and we have a little house and almost don't have enough bread to eat. Our father was in prison for almost one year and there was nobody to take care of us so we had only 50kg of flour. We don't have time to play like other children do.

Tenta

Sing some songs

Sing some songs for children
When I've gone away,
Even this one, maybe,
Though I'm too sad to say
'Goodbye' to the children
We can sometimes sing
Lift the voice in singing
Even with heart-breaking.

Sing some songs for young girls
When I've gone away.
Treat them as gold, treat them as pearls
Treat them as Queens of the May
And they will be kind and reward you
With smiles like the sun shining
And lift the voice in singing
To cheer you on your way.

Sing some songs for young men
When I've gone away,
Treat them with cream, treat them with wine
And praise them as you may.
Laugh back into their laughing eyes
And they will want to sing,
Join in the strenuous singing
The songs you'll sing to the children
When I've gone away.

Jenny Joseph

Pieta

When the thorn was green
my gold-haired son was born.
His birth star blazed between
the midnight and the dawn.

When the thorn was white
new wine flowed: he was wed.
May blossom glowed at night
and graced his marriage bed.

When the thorn was red
they tore his life from me.
The swollen fruit he bled
hung dripping from the tree.

Now the thorn is black
and storm clouds cloak the sky.
Men pray to bring him back;
I only wait to die.

Dickon Abbott

On Seeing a Photograph
of Affan Ramić's Dead Son

'All these moments will be lost in time like tears in rain.'
    – from *Bladerunner*

A new studio. And new work too, light and airy,
After the charred *object trouvé* cross-beams and fiery black conflagrations
Of the siege pieces. A bridge, all creams and whites,

Ultramarine for the Neretva, a touch of terracotta.
At the table, jokingly, he tosses each of us an egg –
Unknown hardboiled. When he opens a new monograph

He's a small prewar boy with his parents, then with a small boy
In summer shorts, aged five forever. As he thumbs on
I am still back with it – or rather, with the face transmogrified

To my own son's. When I mention how sad it is
An eye-rim glistens like must on a summer grape.
A brush on the shoulder. Nothing more. We move on...

Sarajevo outskirts. Leaving again. Past Ilidža –
Its old Austrian tram sign in Roman and Cyrillic – lush midsummer
Bosnian verdure. O radiant day

Booming like the pink-bloomed light
Outside the flytrap window screen of my grandmother's death-room!
Haycocks, maize, woodpiles, ruins, lavender;

Orchards, hill-meadows, an aqueduct, kiosks, turban-stones.
Jars of honey at roadside stalls. Blaze of alpine buttercup. How to bear up,
How go on, when the world's refracted to a single tear?

Chris Agee

Requiem

'Hitler, c'est moi'
    – Glucksmann

Something had turned me back. Broken stone. Ochre and lime
Leaves in the pockmark of a mortarsplash. I paused

To marvel at the chaos that composed them
Impasted in hoarfrost like sperms or dead souls frozen

In the liquid oxygen of time. Then back again
To the smoothness on a mosque's threshold, a revenant

Drifting on in the first flurries of Friday afternoon,
Windless and lightweight, sifting down in grey silence,

I walk on past shawled faces in an old Yugoslav café,
Bread smells and a glimpse of loaves, jars stacked pyramidal

As in Russia, crossing Habsburg tramlines to the market stalls
Where legs and shoe leather move round the small splash

That, invisible, unsought, I wince at. Walnuts, cabbages, tangerines:
Onions, apples, peppers, honeycomb: bowls of cheese, sunflower seeds:

Beautiful, spartan Arcimboldo, where Sarajevo snow is falling, falling...
Is ash falling into the next century.

Chris Agee

Say

Say there were no guns
say war was illegal.
Say no child was ever tortured
in the long scream of a dark cellar.
Say there was no greed:
no-one was hungry, or homeless.
Say we championed dissidents;
say no-one bled alone in midnight alleys.
Say the blind could see
and life-support machines
had taught the almost-dead to dance.
Say Biko and Ken Saro-Wiwa
had never had to exist
and Auschwitz wasn't even a figment.
Say there was no death.
Say we could promise to love one another
forever.
Say fear was as foreign as Mars.

Would we have to invent the dark
as a place in which to hide?
Would we need death?

Roselle Anguin

Box

Tonight I've lost it
at sea in my own blood

dreams awash: Tibet
Tiananmen Falklands Iraq Ireland

too much. Am drowning.
Fingerprints on walls; an outline

marooned on the flagstones.
Which way home? Rome still burning –

though now the fiddle stumbles. Everywhere
a numbing: this wide-blue-eyed

complacency of silence. No-one
remembers how to talk

or what will lay down bridges,
hold us up. Forgetting

how grass grows; what makes
a blackbird, or a spring.

Roselle Anguin

A Hungry Ghost

You may see my photo,
for a fraction of a second
my imprint on the light.
Then I am gone,
a ghost in the forest.

I am reality denied,
eaten by hunger and sores,
chased by an army
that would cut its own throat to kill me.
But for all that
they cannot find me.
I belong nowhere they can reach.

They shot my father where he stood,
took my sisters away,
left my mother to die of grief.
But they missed me.
I ran to the forest.

Now I haunt them.
I will always be here
just where they imagine me,
a demon banging a gong
and hurling the screams of their victims
back at them.
The deeper they come
the more they fear me.
I will drive them mad with their fear.

For though I am a ghost,
I am a hungry ghost
and the people will feed me.

Mike Barlow

The Revolution of Poetry

In a city in a strange country
a young woman sits
in a room full of poets.
It is midwinter.
The raw wind brings
the desert with it.

But in this room
they are wrapped in quilts and laughter,
circled on the floor,
their feet starred to the centre
where the brazier burns.

She will remember this
always,
as she will remember
the poems
that are not about
the mountains and rivers,
beasts strange and ordinary
they describe.
They are poems for friends
who have answered a knock
in the middle of the night,
whose eyes have blazed with dreams
and terror.

Back home again
she recites them in her sleep,
reads letters telling her of change,
of hope.
She sees the news,
the chanting millions
taking to the streets.

She writes.
'At last!' she writes.
She hears nothing.
Her letters disappear
like poets.

Mike Barlow

Inside the Walnut

A little boy goes missing.
Everyone in the village searches for him.

Then the village vanishes
and the boy finds himself alone
in a silence that can't be broken
by his shouts, his cries.

Maybe it's a game, he thinks,
the way grandfather shuffled a pea
beneath walnuts. Now you see it...

The boy tries to carry the whole village
inside him, practises the words
for them, how to speak as one, as many.

He hunts for words where there are none,
long words with feathers,
wingspan of a Cormoran, Chameleon words
that shape themselves to leaves of bread,
warm from the hands that knead to give –
a blanket, a bed, a place far away
from this field of blackbirds.
A word that has no history to repeat
and repeatedly ignore, a place where
old bones lie undisturbed by the new

and all the lost and missing are found
in a moment before the moment
when all the words ran out.

Judi Benson

Exode

Pity for the endless chain of refugees
Whose drained faces
Drift across our TV screens.

They have come so far
Carrying children piggyback.
They've had nothing to eat or drink for days.

Behind them, villages in flames.
But they can't stay here.
The people here are poorer than they are.

We are debating
How to deal with them.
In fifty years perhaps we will know

What we should have done.
So much ignorance, so much misery
And so much hate.

Here is a list of names. Here is the finger
That keeps moving down. Here are the Armies
Of Liberation.

Here the women whose menfolk are missing
Rock babies to sleep in folded blankets,
Here their oldsters drop like flies

And here their youngsters are playing football
With a lopsided bundle (zoom
Goes our eye) of rags and plastic

And adhesive tape. Where did they get tape?
The camera turns over their ball
Like a Stone Age artifact.

Beverley Bie

The Bomber at Bixha

Above Bixha,
the mountains rise through oak forest,
virgin as the day God dropped
the first acorn
upon Albania

In the grey shade,
wolves sleep the just sleep of animals,
who kill to eat then dream
with paws twitching
like hearth dogs'

In a gully,
beyond a windswept bouldered ridge,
rests the tangled corpse
of a bomber posted
lost in '44

In high summer,
the searing stones too hot for hands,
the gearbox oil still seeps
from the bearings
like old blood

It came,
flown by young men with girlfriends,
wives or sisters left behind
to pass the long hours
quietly weeping

In Tirana,
the mullahs were being put to death,
the marble steps of the mosque
of Etham Bey
tinged scarlet

Looking up,
men in darkness surveyed the confident night,
the autumn oaks starting to shed
their leaves like scraps
of impossible peace

Nothing,
neither parachutes nor promises arrived,
only the dull crump of ordnance
like summer thunder
in the mountains

At daybreak,
the partisans climbed up to the place,
finding where fire and death
had split the rocks
and hope died

From here,
you can see almost clear to Kosovo,
over unsullied sylvan mountains
even wild Byron
might still know

On quiet nights
above Bixha, you can almost hear them,
the ghosts of airmen and of partisans
wondering when it
all will end

Note: The bomber at Bixha, a Halifax, exploded on impact with the
mountainside in the last week of October, 1944, whilst on a secret SOE
supply mission to Albanian partisans who were, at the time, engaging the
German army in the Battle of Tirana. The aircraft remains unidentified to this
day. The RAF flight crew were all killed. They have no graves.

Martin Booth

The Field of
the Cloth of Clothes

Patchwork
   stitched with misery
      beautiful motley

Groundcover so intricate
   this patterning of possessions
      puts Jackson Pollock in the shade

Kaleidoscope of colour
   and like that grinding mill
      it means a change of wear

A change of terror
   By night the owners
      were torn away, all 30,000

A favourite sweater rain-soaked
   a child's loved blanket
      someone's checked shirt

Multiply these by thousands
   for each lost garment count
      a suit of suffering

The bright field lies here
   signalling to a god
      who this Easter turns his face

Anne Born

Rivers

Underground their sources rise
overground they make beds
but move unsleeping, flowing
seaward. Everything near them
is nourished and cherished,
rivers are veins through mountains.

Men make bridges. Wars unmake them.
Connections snap, destruction rains.

A house centres and protects,
hold love, routine, dear everydays.
Children. Order. Till someone drops
a glass. Cracks, breaks, slippages start,
water stops in its tracks, and then
a throat is cut; water runs red.

Rivers are splintered, water gives way.
through valleys streams have legs
driven and herded mile after mile.
Day is nightmare, nights are killers.
Serb blood runs hot in Kosovo,
but cold in the ousted, so cold.

Terrors cover the map
and death's in vogue again. Again.
But live hearts creep over borders,
while at home
who can torch most houses,
shoot most backs?

Through the mountains rivers of blood
are men, women, children weeping,
rain falls and veils the crowds
on open hillsides with a cold pall.

Two stretcher bearers stumble uphill,
their burden falls on stony ground
and a sick Sisyphus rolls down.

This is a Balkan spring. In Europe.
A lost child, Kosovo, cries and cries.

Anne Born

It gets late early

The years pass quietly. Success does not
complete the garden. You stand inside
your storms, plotting your own borders,
exposed to the atmosphere's equilibrium.

Light spills from morning to night, changes
your face, hidden behind layers of tangled words.
It gets late early. Your feet leave. Looking back,
it's hard to think of you as a stranger.

People, like petals, seem to fall mostly at night.

Andy Brown

How old is the light

Before we can discuss eternity
gravity lengthens the day. Imagine
the limitless space; a football high
in the air above the players' heads;

the so-called *paradox* of infinity.
You could almost quote the Biblical
statement 'Nothing can be said'
& prove it in the open field of days.

All you have to do is correct the
amounts of light. One assumes
& why not? It's only logical to
assume it's logical to think

although we know this can't be true –
the earth is made up. The key
to understanding the complex lies
in singling out the stars by eye.

Come close to the sun, face to face
with its processes. Look at what
goes on in dying, ask: How does
a dead star look, how old is the light?

Andy Brown

After Alcuin
on the Sacking of Lindisfarne

Our fields we leave waste
earth bankrupt
in pain for children lost
to stealth and bad faith

Ruled by chance and death
each in our time
denied our grief, no privacy
in this brute casual world

Homes desolate, shamed,
memories broken, frailty
questioning what
cant be known

Perhaps elsewhere there's peace
– but not here, lost, lost in
this worlds
swirling tides forever

Laid low who once was free
in rags who once was proud
eyes dim who once was clear
weak, famished who once was strong

A small voice by your ear
clear as a trumpet
as we turn
sick from the burning world

And so we change
and so everything moves on
and so what remains elsewhere is
uninterrupted day

Richard Caddel

Bentham Twinned with Racak

In a village like mine they come by night,
boot in the doors, drag the young men –
and boys – from their beds and march them,
hands on heads, half-drunk with sleep
up Robin Lane to the golf course,
line them up on the green
and shoot them one by one in the head.

Next day observers come in orange jeeps, take notes
and number the bodies lying face down in the bunker.
The rain runs red through sand and women wail
in Bentham-twinned-with-Racak.

Phoebe Caldwell

Good Friday 1999

it was the sound of a bird
startled from sleep its wings hurting the air

it was a sound like shame
since then I have not slept

my ears multiplied I heard the hammers
ringing down the weeping of men and women

the wing of sorrow
beating louder and louder

words betray its delicacies
which hide in each freckle of each face

each gesture each strand of hair each voice
calling its own call like no other

it is the shadow of love
kicked bleeding from the garden

whose hands burn
through barricades of flame

Alison Croggon

Landscape with Rocks

They say that everything has a song for itself.
You pause at the gates of a cemetery
with a song in your heart
though it seems that it's drunken singing
rather than the other kind which you associate
with the red throats of birds
or after the shooting stops.

And if there are songs for asbestos and ball bearings
there is music, too, for a funeral;
steep hills have a rhythmic accompaniment
and so does water in a pail.

So here's to the rolling of rivers and tyres
and here's to a song about global warming
and the last remaining leg of the chair
thrown onto the real log fire.

Here's to the knock at the door
and the Croatian phrasebook sent in the mail,
the way he opened it, read the instructions,
slipped it into his pocket and began to dance
the dance of his furious ancestors
(they all baked heavy cake
and painted wings on dark-skinned madonnas).

And here's to the song he sang
the night he went out like a light
and knocked on his neighbour's door,
a song for the men who took everything
and confessed to nothing.

Everything, they say, has a song, a signature,
a difficult second album.

From the firm signature at the end of a letter,
the one that ends in heavy artillery,
to a walk through the flower market at midnight
and the red spot that grew on her cheek,
the way no one spoke for several minutes
and how he filled a black bag then ceased to exist.

A military truck found abandoned a few miles from the airport.
It was in the way she did her face in the mirror,
only harder this time, and with rocks.

How the job she took as a paid companion
turned bad then worse
and *The History of Magnetic Attraction*
with illustrations, spiral bound,
made a disappointing Xmas gift.

Her dead husband was sitting drunk under the tree
splitting his seams
and waving his chequebook stubs
as if they were a flag of surrender
and surrender he did

in public, in private, in state
and finally wherever he got the opportunity

for laughing under pressure
and turning off the lights
and cutting the line from his hands to his mouth,
for taping up the doors and windows

for the cross made of the number plates of crashed cars
and for not confusing willingness with capability.

He was seen elbowing into some one else's picture
and dreaming under gas,

He was found laughing at things you can't forget
and pointing at things you never laugh at.

There was a spider in the box of matches that burst into flame in his pocket.

He woke at dawn
with a glass of heavy brandy
miraculously upright in his outstretched hand.
A small crowd of people
stood singing through the shattered windows

and when the last were carried away
the men in uniform cursed themselves
for not getting it right the first time,
for not getting it right in the end.

Tim Cumming

Snow

It is the nineteenth century, and it is snowing.
You're wearing a long overcoat and heavy black shoes
and ahead of you the future's a white sheet
over antique furniture before an auction
of all your effects, including even
your posture, temper and appetite
and what you're thinking of is food,
steaming plates of everything in a room
you've built with postcards of the view
from the best years of your life
but you're late and your past is catching up with you.

The new diseases are knitting their clothes in the cellar
and everyone ahead of you's asleep or hanging curtains.
The gas light in the stairwell is a great fall of snow,
and from this you press and peel off the imprint
of families living five to a room
at thousands of different points in history,
and the effects of interior light.
It is morning. You are late. Somebody has spilled the milk.
Concorde and the noise bomb are busy being invented
and the bus lane is just around the corner
behind the gasometer. Camps of all kinds
are establishing themselves on the horizon,
on television. You can see their fires, spill their beans,
walk their moonwalk. The air smells of burning fat,
but this is progress and you are late. You can't stop.
The future's behind you, and ahead of you the past

Tim Cumming

Lullaby
A woman speaks

To another country you've been taken.
How soundly do you sleep?
What language must you learn on waking?
I don't know when you weep.

My old, suede-soft, homely darkness
was lit by your piercing scream.
– Last night, did you see a different starscape
when I cradle you in dream?

Peter Dale

The News (1950-1999)

The moment full for all of us
Not as it was when it was merely
Of itself   Moon over harvest
Large   The true self gathered there

We looked and saw a world
The world with care might win
Our eye immediate to its need
Unqualified   A harvest home

Now there's a mass of distant fires
Too many words that want for mind
A dark smoke down to see
We do not find ourselves lay hands

On precious things   Long nights
Of stars we look right through
The stations calling calling   Straw
Of old fields trampled underfoot

Peter Dent

A text about a spring

I dissolved
And streamed

Streamwards

Riverwards

Seawards

Now here I am

Now here I am
Without myself

Bitter

How can I go back
To whence I sprang?

Mak Dizdar (Bosnia)
translated by Francis R. Jones

A text about the five

Four men leading one man bound
One man whom the four men hound

Four men's faces dour and dire
Over water over wire

On they scoff and on they trough
Through each thread and through their bread

Through each hedge and through each Y
Until freedom us untie

Past the homes and past the tombs
Through the earth and through the sky

Four men leading one man bound
One man whom the four men hound

One man counted bound and led
One man whom the four men dread

Mak Dizdar (Bosnia)
translated by Francis R. Jones

Wave Ghazal

This boy is in love with Maria
he wears a wedding ring on the wrong finger

Satellite dishes scan the troposphere
For voices warm with promise

When he finishes the fighting
He is going to Belgrade to marry her

The industrial palaces are crumbling
Voices die mutate their rays

Of dark intentionality flicker resonate
In blood bone muscle in the cathedrals

On the floor of his truck
His Kalashnikov points into the trees

Too many voices call mutate the *duende*
In the quantum void

The convoy's trucks clatter through the forest
On a mountain road he hears

The *duende*'s long bow wave
On the receiving station

And somewhere there's a house
Made of blond wood filmed with dust

The spirit in that house the
Spiral in the dust

Ken Edwards

Stealth

they cannot be seen
in their black
and angled wings

a darkness to bounce
back probing beams

but the reds, yellows
and blues of those
other moving things

who trudge because
they have no wings

are watched by
snow and rain because
they can be seen

and look to the air
for greater things

but what will not be seen
is distant black
and protecting

above the snow and rain
where some think a
god should have been

Mike Ferguson

```
kosovo (population 1.6 million), of great historic importance
kosovo (population 1.6 million), of great historic importance
kosovo (population 1.6 million), of great historic importance
kosovo (population 1.6 million), of gr at historic importance
kosovo (population 1.6 million), of gr at historic importance
kosovo (population 1.6 million), of gr at historic importance
kosovo (pop lation 1.6 million), of gr at historic importance
kosovo (pop lation 1.6 million), of gr at hi toric importance
kosovo (pop lation 1.6 million), of gr at hi toric im ortance
kos vo (po  lat on 1.6 mil ion), of gr at hi toric im ortan e
ko  vo (po  lat on 1.6 m l ion), of gr at hi toric im or an e
ko  vo  o  lat on 1.6 m l ion), of g  at hi toric i  or an e
ko  o   o  lat on 1.6 m     ion), of g  at hi t  ic i  or an e
k   o   o  lat on 1.6 m     ion),  f g  at hi t  ic i  or  n e
k   o   o  l   on 1.6 m     ion),  f g  at hi t  ic i  or    e
k   o   o  l   o  1.6 m     on),   f     at hi t  ic i  or    e
k   o      o  1.5 m     on),   f     at hi t  ic i  or    e
k   o   .  o  1.5       on),   f        hi t  ic i     r    e
k   o         1.4       on),   f        hi t  i  i     r    e
k   o         1.3       on),   f        hi t  i  i     r    e
k   o         1.1       o ),   f        hi t  i  i     r    e
k   o         0.9       o ),   f        hi t  i  i          e
k   o         0.7       o ),            hi t  i  i          e
    o         0.4       o   ,           hi t  i  i          e
    o         0.3           ,           hi t  i  i
    o         0.2           ,           hi t     i
              0.1           ,           hi t
              0.0           ,           hi t
              0.0           ,
              0.0           ,
              0.0           ,
              0.0
              0.0
              0.0
               .0
               .0
               .0
                0
                0
                0
```

Peter Finch

A

A man is running and his house is on fire
and we are in our gardens
using the words we always sing.

A man is running and his house and his dog are on fire
and we say enter our house
and we will let you enter our dance.

A man is running and his house and his dog and his children are on fire
and we say hear our prayers and here
is a hymn so sit down and quiet.

A man is running and his house and his dog and his children and his bed
are on fire are on fire
and the birds are burning also and the small church by the lake
and the grandfather clock and the place where he hid his letters;

and we are saying come in and dance the prayer with us
and say the songs that we all make true
and we will share our sounds and give you our silences
and so you will be still.

A man is running in the stillness of the house
and in the silence of the hurt dog
and in the sounding of the children
and in the doing of the garden;

and we are all immortal in his intent
and we are all now running in his meaning
and we are all now becoming in his words.

His silence sits on the mantel with the flowers,
his silence occupies a new place at the table,
his silence ascends the stairs to the little bedroom,
his silence rattles in the early morning bathroom.

His silence occupies our house
and will and will

and will.

David H. W. Grubb

Game

Dusk taking over a court among conifers
though still discernible in thickening shadows
the ghostly tennis-ball and two boys in white flannels
whose dogged exchanges continuing voiceless
let the bored parents pacing back hand in hand
over the sweet-smelling layer of pine-needles
smile in collusion at that stubborn intention
to have done with the set before succumbing to darkness

All four are dead now. War. Then sorrow. The net
sags as a frontier between tufts of ragweed.
Gossamer drifts where victor and loser
stood preparing to serve. Well below earshot
welcoming gunfire waited over the water
where the bone huntsman got ready to barter
a wad of black telegrams for broken athletes.

Upstairs in the shrine put up during mourning
tasselled caps hang fading by a vixen's paw
dust-greyed now gummed to its wooden shield.
In blurred team-photographs beardless features
recede year by year from their side of the glass.
No-one flicks cobwebs from the prongs of antlers.
On one varnished oar nailed dry to the wall
a roll-call formed a triumphant ladder of gold.
The date has faded. Each bright initial is tarnished.

Harry Guest

Map

for Tomaz Salamun

My nation is a pasture horseless in demeanor.
Its contours ignite happenstance from harm-
lessness less distant in manner.
Thrush appointed to hold truck with the pasture
nourish the pasture.
Shares hired to counsel the pasture
thresh the pasture.
When the shape of the sound stripping the wind
builds a wall at the edge of the pasture,
it rehearses last rites
for this burden drained by distance.

Walllessness should not be considered a harm
or lack, but a willingness to counsel
and receive counsel from horses
in a horseless nation,
where the pasture remains as reminder, reminding
the horses of what's remained
and what remains for the horses.

Brian Henry

A shattered honeycomb

To the ruins of my grandparents' house in Plehan

Keep me in your atmosphere Orion
I'm coming with a seashell of well-hemmed words
Words which bear drowsily quivering linden trees
whose coronets of blossoms in the breeze
draw the figures of my solitude
A long wall with my grandfather's beekeeping hat
carved as it were into the marble facing
My father's laughter preserved
pinkish blue in the corners of the room
swathes my arms like silken velvet

Keep me in your atmosphere Orion
I'm coming with a seashell of well-hemmed words
Words which bear the dense heavy folds of dark
from which eternity issues forth
and to which it returns
Ruins whose dust is the sole certainty
                                    of what is to come
As your hourglass sets great processions of nations
moving off into timelessness Orion
and these terrible times of death
the omnipresent

Aneta Benac Krstić (Bosnia)
translated by Francis R. Jones

Threads

On only one
of the endless skein of slender threads
which you shape into
a colour, a word, a dream and a love
and then assemble into a sense
and a new world on white
do our lives depend

Sometimes you'll weave them into masts and sails
for a boat in which you take me out to the cape
for only up there can its whole
expanse and depth be seen

Today in the space of your eyes
I see a line of deaths
improvised from the things I touch in this room

Aneta Benac Krstić (Bosnia)
translated by Francis R. Jones

Elegy

to reduce one's life to a favourite book full of cuttings, photos, mementoes, and one or two watercolours by a lover; a book small enough to carry with you everywhere

to live for the moment, needing no more than daily being; to breathe in the sunlight and walk among trees, to love the people you are with; to be content; to trace one's finger in the dust

to die alone in the dark, swimming toward the light... afraid but not afraid; remembering a promise you once made

to desire the moment, to seek the light; to let judgement and memory go

to trace one's finger in the dust, shake the sand from one's shoes; to turn and meet the day

to know the morning is coming, to smile in the dark while waiting for the dawn

to converse with strangers and not despise your differences; to love the people you are with for exactly who they are

to sing in the dusk, to pray in the morning; to stay silent and drive on beside the talkative one who always needs to speak

to die alone in the dark, singing about the light; dreadfully afraid, able to remember nothing of except a promise you once made

to leave one's life behind like a book, pages fluttering in the breeze, fading in the sun; photos and cuttings lost for ever or treasured by a lover

to let one's life become dust; to turn and face the light

Rupert M Loydell

Continuum

This April morning is dark,
bluer and colder than yesterday.
However, the scene will change.

An unusual collection of creeps, freaks
and divinely accented characters
are outside making history.

They used to look hostile,
never said anything much;
we just shuffled around them.

There never was any ill feeling;
I found something admirable
about their hanging-on to life.

Sound begins to come from somewhere –
an outcry of birds, the barking of dogs,
a grinding that has music hidden deep within.

What else do we have to listen to?
The noise of heat walking around the walls
after the summer has gone into silence.

Rupert M Loydell

Landscapes: Memories

Gable ends stare empty at the sky.
The apples rot where they have fallen,
by burned stumps and broken brick.
A grey light metals inland water, blank
mirror, cross-hatched with beds of reed.

Fields and hills retain long memories –
tower of the stolen bride, the bridge where
twenty warriors were slain. Stories cling
down slow centuries of birth and death,
routines of husbandry, eyes rarely lifted
from the soil. But then the clearances:
roofs broken open to the hungry wind;
no one at home to name an empty land.

In distant cities, memory of a stranger slips
between two paving stones. Sweat-shop
and transit camp are quickly bulldozed.
Shopping centres, tower blocks, carry the names
of farms or orchards. Ghosts choke on traffic fumes.
Rumour alone may linger of a burial pit,
an alleyway where throats were slit.

Blood cries out from the ground, but
other noises clamour in the ear. The view
shuts down to roundabouts, or some dark stairwell,
colonized by newer and more urgent passions,
haunted with all too present fears.

Tony Lucas

Up Country

The scarecrow in a boiler suit,
with arms akimbo, white cloth helmet,
startled me, if not the birds,
coming across the ridge to see
some baled-out pilot, drunken
motorcyclist, propped up and waiting.

Great flints lie scattered all across
this field, like broken skulls
and bones, ploughed up from some
dire battle, not so long ago.
Over the hill, a shotgun bangs at crows.

All down the hedge, huge flies
like helicopters, hover to attack.
The farmer and his land have signed
no truce. They warn us that
a few hours of spring sunshine
can be taken as no pledge of peace.

Tony Lucas

No, not even death
can interrupt the charity,
the green glance of tourmaline
that streams mute and immortal
like the light of eyes
that look with equal peace
on markets and basilicas.

Not even death, though
he's rehearsed the break-in
just as often as
grains have blown,
green blades have lifted.

He is foiled by birth
and lurks in the sierras
of his strategy
where his tactic is surprise.

And we live in the uplands
of our imperishable life,
where the phoenix feeds on
frankincense
a full five hundred years.

Gabriel Millar

For Akhmatova

Far from the Neva, and the melancholy
of the old things going,
leagues from the grief of the one
who would not emigrate,
whose lids were at half-mast for
the perpetual funeral of romance,
and the fast passing of innocence –

it is different here:
no snow after Easter –
the birds were muffled by the grave
in Komarovo.
Here the drama is more domestic:
the heroine is celluloid, and has a hero
who does not die for his truth,
or even live by it.
There is no knock in the night.

No, here the soul is purloined away slowly
by superpowers smiling like saviours.
The craven grab at pleasure has replaced
the noble joy of having backbone,
and the lift of freedom.
For a mess of pottage we have done
what Akhmatova would never do:
we have sold our sacred essence,
we have sold our song.

Gabriel Millar

Square One

There is blood on our hands
as this era's dusk descends,
as its twilight is marked
by our return, full-cycle,
to where we began
and from where we learned little,
instead, idling on indifference,
trusting it all to have gone away.

The dead have been woken
to walk with the ghosts
of uncomfortably familiar dogma
upon uncomfortably familiar territory,
upon an untamed tillage of torment
from which the only profit falls
to those whose plagued steel
is the ploughshare refashioned to kill.

In our myopia, we have
celebrated the end of that which
has brought us back to begin again;
these crystals of ice, that held
so much together, we believed
to be there only to be thawed,
to be exchanged for the flow
of flux, ignorant of its unseen terror.

We have found ourselves caught
between a devil and the deep
blue sea, with what must be done
being done, but being done
only now the graffiti has dried,
the writing left so long unread
as to engender culpability
as an onus to be somehow shared.

John Mingay

Talismans

Pocket the stone
your mother made soup from,
press the last leaf
of the family tree,
pinch thin air
between your fingers,
pass into life
unharmed and free.

Sharpen the blade
your father fashioned,
sound the first note
on the messenger's horn,
sift fine gold
through a broken hourglass,
search for the rose
which has no thorn.

John Mole

Magnolia

Storm-stripped wings
of magnolia
litter the ground.

Too late
to think better of it
the season
takes what's coming.

Stumbling over
scattered limbs
a mother
carries her child.

No words for this –
only the silence
of each open mouth

John Mole

Ambiguous Peace

A strimmer and a distant aircraft,
the sound of daft, greedy gulls –
these fill the silent spinning air
with what noise there is this noon,

and thought is like a deep-laid plan
of some lost river. Sure, this is
what it must be like to dream
heaven's boredom or to be imprisoned.

All the world over there is delight
and wretchedness, and a longing
for elusive peace. But the waterdrop
that hits a tree's stiff leaf

and splatters like an ending star,
the wrong one does another, or
the surprise of joy that comes like sun
thrill, break peace, make thoughts run now
                    and always.

William Oxley

The Great Mess

I walk past the gathering of shops
in a pedestrian precinct, and
there's the sun above the great tops
of grown-up buildings, a shining CD

of gold. And – O my streetwise angel –
faces reflect the great mess
in which devils of emotion wrangle
now that we have come to this his

last decade of doom and despair.
Alright, so prices dance up and down
and whingers tear at their hair,
but still there was certainty once

like a feather of hope in the air.
So maybe tomorrow or after
something may turn up somehow?
After all, I'm one for belief and laughter
like you – and for the hereafter.

William Oxley

Chosen People

Lord, you are my Lord, and my enemy's.
He looks like you, and names you in his prayer
as I do in whose gut the venom is.
You hang upon his wall, perfume his lair.

Through our contention you are torn in two,
yet in your suffering reach out to each.
Why do I let the enemy fill my view
when I could see you standing in the breach,

the antidote to our hate, reconciling
twin worlds of us, twin anger thrust with fear,
contrariness and Shimei-like reviling

a Hillel's gentleness and the austere
God of the burning spirit, with the smiling
countenance through my enemy made clear?

Brian Louis Pearce

Call it Street Stubbornness

Never dismissed this service, always counted
in the muster of your forces, posted
to duties still demanding all our powers
on the outskirts of your empire, hours
from anywhere, half-starved, the sand the same
blinder for leagues, still serving in your name,
although we feel abandoned, know the pain
of being forgotten, not to meet again;
though orders have long ceased to reach us and
no one believes relief will come to hand;
though given up by all, in our frail party
some inmost stubborn streak's still feeling hearty.
The fact is that this regiment won't give up
if it has been disbanded, sold a pup.
What you have once created can't be stood
down and our enlistment is for good.
Our confidence is this, that what the cold
hard world wrote off, you in your cause enrolled.
We choose to trust in that and your control
whether or not you leave us in this hole.

Brian Louis Pearce

Kosovo

The hollowed heart of Europe
Clenched like a fist

That one man – like a steel bullet –
Can break so many hearts

And we must stop him
Stop this

– stop what?

The one crime we can commit
To fail to recognise
That everything is our sister and brother,
And then to kill it

Till the world shrinks
To the size of our insignificance
– a polluted irritant in the eye of God –

A dream down the wrong end of a telescope
Become our fashionable fragmented nightmare

And it's only by filling our hearts up from the inside
With love and rage

That we can say No – or Yes – loudly enough
To see our world whole again.

Jay Ramsay

Song for the outward journey

Beneath the bridge, through the tunnel,
in a forward-facing seat, leave.
The buzzing lines to anywhere will hold you.

The wiry grass that clings to hills
will shiver in the fields tonight.
The land you left behind today will hold you.

The brooks will swell and burst their banks
to carve out shapes that you won't read.
The native mud still on your boots will hold you.

Ironic birds swoop down to wink,
remind you of unsaid goodbyes.
The sky you thought as grey and void will hold you.

So magpies croon and croak so they can hold you
and trees sway bare and brown and stretch to hold you
and hedges mime a wind-blown grief
as bridges creak, moan, sway and keen
cross rivers dashing seawards trying to hold you,
from a place that holds its breath but cannot hold you.

Mark Robinson

Variations on William Carlos Williams

I'm sorry, I have eaten the stones you fought so fiercely for.
They smelt so much like bread
and were so filling. You will find more.

I'm sorry, we have cut off the water supply.
You will be better off without it.
It would only have reminded you.

I'm sorry, we have murdered your mother,
father, husband, three of your four sons and your daughter.
They are in a better place.

I'm sorry, we have burnt out your house.
The flames looked beautiful against the dark sky,
and the few bricks standing have a kind of grandeur.

I'm sorry, we have allocated your territory
to someone who will use it better.
It was never what you needed, or wanted really.

I'm sorry, the pictures on your walls
have been translated into ashes. They were cheap,
and never really gave the impression you hoped.

I'm sorry you have to go. It was probably time.
The morning was so fresh and new,
and the neighbourhood not what it was.

I'm sorry. I am sorry.
No, really, I am. I'm sorry.
Listen. I am sorry. Listen.

I'm sorry, we have decided to give you your freedom.
You will enjoy it, it is so sweet and precious,
and lasts longer than a single lifetime.

Mark Robinson

Points of Light

'Tell me again about Europe and her pains...'
 – William Empson, 'Aubade'

Through this screen of trees,
a thicker darkness than the night's,
come glinting flashes –

74

lights in windows, cars
negotiating backstreets
or streetlamps themselves.

If I move, they blur,
bleed into one another
like blasts seen through tears

from a further war,
signals in blockaded gulfs,
black-out violations...

Now horizons glow;
our children are still snoring
and the flat is calm.

Peter Robinson

The End

Never mind my actual death,
my actuarial death will be
in two thousand and thirty.

The Maldives will have drowned
and the rich will have migrated
to temperate Siberia and northern Canada.

Opportunist scrub will have invaded
dieback forest, and leafhoppers will have
eradicated potatoes in a one-season plague.

No creature will swim in the planktonless seas.
Birds will have failed to return long since,
and none of the seasons come round any more.

At the rate of three an hour I cannot calculate
how many species will have gone. Ours will hang on,
though the poor will be poorer, and blistered.

You'd think I'd be glad to be done:
but I should have liked to hear the last stutter of self,
to know whether extinction comes from heat or starvation or war

and whether everyone goes on saying that something
should be done: it will be like starting the final chapter
with the last few pages torn out.

Jane Routh

from History or Sleep

C20th Blues 31

This poem was written during a similar, but distinct, war and humanitarian crisis in 1995. While history never dies, and poetry may be attempted testimony, I had hoped not to witness approximate reinactment in the present, when the poem becomes so effectively useless, unless read, against its own grain, as prophecy. 10 April 1999

One raped
can another relax
stroke
orgasmic dead fur
from this catalogue of
terror, frog-eyed navigators
chart us
while enemies invade
(liberate) equivocal
loyalty
tells us we cannot afford
to open the window
you cannot see
another's sorrow without
hanging
on the breeze, a counter

to think and feel
pleasure empty
as a mouth willing cool
scarecrows itself
replaces
all with its fevered dreams
of possible tomorrows
bark
you wake (your victim
pours from you
virtual memories conflate
occasions
dissolve
salt sweat stains
to find – who? – dead)
the recognition that
another human being has responded

haunts

Robert Sheppard

Picasso is Right

On my bedroom wall
Father paints a beautiful picture
of the famous river that runs beside our house.

The river is black and all the clouds,
fields, thin shimmering houses, stars,
moons and bridges are black, cool and noir.
Soon the entire wall is black.

His river-painting is so beautifully black,
so wild, so percussive,
it makes me weep, on each of my tears
is painted a tiny curled-up baby, seahorse-neat.

Father shrugs off my praise.
'Picasso is right,' says Father,
'black is the only colour.
You can fly through black!'

'But, Father, where shall we fly?'
Father smiles and looks wise.
'To one of the smaller Slavic countries,
of course,' he cries,

'where they have chosen black
out of all the colours that are...
the colour that makes everyone weep...'

Penelope Shuttle

Imagining the Worst

A bullet with my name on it!

This morning clacking shears
rattled a sick-bear's bandaged head
of wasps. The secret life of hedges!
I had stumbled on warlords muttering.

A million bullets in a war to kill a man!

Dive-bombed, strafed,
I fell through clouds of pollen,
smacked between the eyes.

Matt Simpson

Trillium

There was a girl screaming on the mountain
over there. All night. She'd gone crazy.

Columns of those driven out. Clips of film.
Photographs of the world's unravelling,
the scattered dead, a city of crows and collateral damage
and dust.   And the silence.

I was in the woods, they shot at me,
I didn't know my way.

Snatches of speech on the airwaves: *help us.*
In such times only hurried notes,
moving to no conclusion, a fool's work
to make anything of them, a liar's to make nothing.

I didn't know my way.
Screaming on the mountain.

The shorthand of death and desolation-
estimates, statistics.   Not a song,
not a poem, not a melody, not a fugue.
Not a single note of any music.

They shot at me I didn't know my way.
There was a girl screaming on the mountain.

Among the trees the wandering white trillium of her headscarf.

Ken Smith

Zagreb: Eating Dog

A concrete road segregates
those shoppers in crocodile shoes
from a hedge of refugees pushing prams

who change at the flick of a red light
into swarms of bees around
Mercedes and BMWs,
which rev up, ready for the escape.

A young mother dodging cars:
like a duck in a shooting range, chancing her luck
for the dead dog whose eyes bulge its last look
and its crimson tongue
tastes a final lick.

Mouths to feed, she humps it back
to her pram.

Peter Street

Zagreb Camp

Our wagons rock, jerk
through lines of potholes
a foot deep in a cinder path
where children walk barefoot.

It's a ride down
into something I don't understand;
a dog shelter where at least
one hundred families live,

who beg out their hands
and cough loud barking coughs.

Naked kids swapping boredom
for disease under a tap
that's splashing cold silver
into mud pies.

Our interpreter – an English Lit. student,
his family wiped out,
is talking of Shelley in a waste land
such as Eliot never saw.

Peter Street

The Gods of Tiepolo

Sometimes when you look up on a bright day,
the clouds have drawn apart, exposing a blue
that, for the moment, you can almost look through.
You're surveying a stage long after the play
has finished. Above you, Tiepolo
presents a weightless mass of gods and legs
in endless apotheosis, delicate as eggs
in a cup, or naked skin in an afterglow
when legs and arms float off into half-sleep
and breasts settle warmly against the ribcage
slipping vaguely down its slopes, while the flat
lower belly shimmers and fingers keep
curling and uncurling like an open page
in a slight breeze. But you can imagine that.

So you imagine it. Although this is
the soft sell version, somewhere beyond which
the world is singing at a sharper pitch,
its shrieks full of glass, crowded with casualties:
men in ridiculous wigs, women with waists
pinched to a tight ring, thin children in beds
with soiled sheets, the poor with their shaved heads
and hollow eyes, cruel sexual gymnasts

one step from madness, new forms of rough trade,
a puritan hell which no amount of light
can keep from sinking deeper into flames.
Imagine it. And through that? The betrayed
clear blue of something very simple, as trite
as tears or touch: the sound of common names.

George Szirtes

Disaster Zone

During the first forty-eight hours
our televison screens revealed
unforgettable scenes of devastation.
We had glimpses through the brown smoke
of a ruined landscape, vaguely reminiscent
of a battlefield from the First World War.
We saw the jagged remains of houses,
the roads engulfed with rubble and littered
with corpses. And once there were close-ups
of a ragged group of dazed and injured children,

apparently unattended and quietly whimpering.
On the third day we were informed
that further television coverage
of the situation in the Disaster Zone
would not be possible. No reason was given,
but a few hours later the radio
bulletins from the region also ceased.
People endeavouring to communicate
by telephone with friends and relatives
inside the Zone had already discovered
that all the lines were dead. It was thus
no longer possible to observe
the appalling desolation or to hear
the anguish of those pleading for assistance.

Raymond Tong

Searching for Snow

Press your nose against the pane,
wish for it. Scan the sky. Listen
for the silence of every living thing
braced against the cold.

You want snowmen, snowball contests,
to be snowed in, kept off school.

Some hope, except in dreams
of dragging caked mittens from tingling fingers,
sipping hot chocolate, regressing to 'Watch With Mother'.

Like a feather bed newly spread with clean sheets
snow remakes the world for however long it lasts
until the tension goes out of it. As childish
as innocence before grown-up boots stamp it out.

Angela Topping

Memory Loss

Heaven must be like this
A flying dog in place of the moon,
Three white-gowned girls
Each twinned in the blue water.

The nurse told me to wait here.
As I wait I dream of the night.
The breakfast fish is as yellow
As Sunday in the golden light.

A bowl of mist stirs in the valley
Even the trees are crumbling
A blaze of pink hurts my eyes.
The devil is pink and smells of roses.

Angela Topping

Late Autumn in Belgrade

(variations on themes of Marina Tsvetaeva)

Not autumn –
Winter is tearing me apart

My fingers –
are colder than my heart

And not just the Sun –
Even the darkness is setting
behind the hill

A single thought –
without a knife can kill

It's not a broiling heat –
But a huge crystal of snow
mysteriously moonlit

And not the garden –
But the livid ghosts of the night

Is this a death?
Or does morning bring light?

Dubravka Velāševic̀

Summa Summarum

The leaves of the ilex by the graveyard
Whipser prophetically.

And barley-corn ripens
Like those actors who
In the same role for a hundredth time

Stand forth before the audience.

Yet do not extol,
To the skies, your native land.
It ought to extol you.

Seen from this cloud
These meadows and fields
Are a stamp album;

And to the ant a smoke ring
Twirling from your cigarette
Is a whole new landscape!

And stop threatening for once
To return next time
To this handful of land without history
Only in the shape of a rider in bronze.

And before you leave
Stroke the bark of these trees
Which all the while have given you
Free lessons in standing tall!

Marko Vešović (Sarejevo)
translated from the Bosnian by Chris Agee

Ampersonata
for Scott Lindsey & i.m. Yulia Zelmanovich (1971-1998)

& day not breaking but already broken

& someone holding another to privilege day

& beauty is for the living, at the perimeter, not the last

& look, so quiet we hear each other think

& a lake that fell off the edge of the eye

& clearing away the rubble, & clearing away the rubble

& days of grace, moments of anguish of course

& I don't understand, I understand

& praise without & do not look back

& call it leaving the lights off, or leaving the lake for another lake

& accommodate the feint & forfeiture, & do not look

& nothing else will trade places again

& not only waving but waving again & except

& what will never be seen, never known at the edge of the eye

& water purling in carets to cover the mirror

& memoirs of air & memoirs of

& eavesdropping on the eyelids of morning

& light & less than light--

    even so, even so

    Andrew Zawacki

Let There Be No War

A war is a cruel word
nobody loves it
a war is a deep wound
which is painful forever

There have been many
little orphans
who know no more
for childish jokes

All people are the same
of flesh and blood,
let he be punished
who war starts the first

Let there be flowers sown
all around the world
and let the children blossom
in joy and happiness

We don't want ever
to be a war again
let it be written
in history only

Every child wants
to dream peacefully
and to play
some new games tomorrow

Every child needs a mum
and a dad too,
Let us all shout out
LET THERE BE NO WAR.

Nela (Kosova; 8 years)

A spell

From the horrors of the night
Daylight wake you.
From paralysis of fear
Action shake you.

From the cruelty within
May love protect you.
Of the uncharity of sin
Let none suspect you.

Against the feverish clutch of greed
Pray kindness ward you,
And your care for those in need
Help to safeguard you.

May your smile divert the stare
That attacks you;
With anxious people everywhere
Let peace relax you.

Jenny Joseph